Tyne & Wear Poets

Edited By Lawrence Smith

First published in Great Britain in 2018 by:

 Young**Writers**

Young Writers
Remus House
Coltsfoot Drive
Peterborough
PE2 9BF
Telephone: 01733 890066
Website: www.youngwriters.co.uk

FOREWORD

Young Writers was established in 1991, dedicated to encouraging reading and creative writing in young people. Our nationwide writing initiatives are designed to inspire ideas and give pupils the incentive to write, and in turn develop literacy skills and confidence, whilst participating in a fun, imaginative activity.

Few things are more encouraging for the aspiring writer than seeing their own work in print, so we are proud that our anthologies are able to give young authors this unique sense of confidence and pride in their abilities.

For our latest competition, Rhymecraft, primary school pupils were asked to enter a land of poetry where they used poetic techniques such as rhyme, simile and alliteration to bring their ideas to life. The result is an entertaining and imaginative anthology which will make a charming keepsake for years to come.

Each poem showcases the creativity and talent of these budding new writers as they learn the skills of writing, and we hope you are as entertained by them as we are.

CONTENTS

Owen Noble (8)	56
Ben Lusby (7)	58
Lily Donaldson (7)	60
Thomas Galbarth (8)	62
Otis Arkley (8)	64
Isabella Peacock (7)	66
Benjamin Clark (8)	68
Ava Fox (7)	70
Luca Zakaidze (8)	72
Max Kelly (7)	74
Euan McDermott (7)	76
Alexandra Mia Wood (8)	77
Florence Hodgetts (8)	78
Matthew Jackson (8)	79
Abbie Rochester (8)	80
Joshua Burton (7)	82
Harry Naill Richardson (7)	83
Kyle Austin (8)	84
George Wallace (8)	85
Amy Brown (8)	86
Luke Gray (7)	87
Jack Warnaby (7)	88
Sophie Rose Bell (8)	89
Madeleine Mae Copus (7)	90
Imilia Young (8)	91
Zahra Ellen Roxby (7)	92
Owen Taylor Short (7)	93
Ollie Bennett (8)	94
Abigail Fox (8)	95
Anya Grace Clayton (7)	96
Molly Imogen Greenwood (7)	97
Kophie Ellen Mckay (7)	98
Abbie Mary Robertson (8)	99
Heidi Cooke (7)	100
Maria Efthimia Kontou-Watson (7)	101
Harry-Thomas Storey (8)	102
Ava Sofia Henderson (8)	103
Riley Lucas Smith (8)	104
Harry Nordstrom Nellis (7)	105
Evie Hedley (7)	106
Marcie Laidler (8)	107
Sophie Potts (7)	108

Lauren Bunting (7)	109
Tom Eron Tindle (8)	110
Katie Reid (7)	111
Abbie McIlwraith (7)	112
Owen Lanaghan (8)	113
Sophie Ann Frater (8)	114
Amelie Jones (7)	115
Zac Alexander Johnson (8)	116
Ben Kernen (7)	117
Grace Connor (8)	118
Ruby Rose Skaife (8)	119
Nola Thompson (8)	120
Amber Howey (8)	121
Katelyn Dowling (7)	122
William Theodore Carson (7)	123
Sam Oxberry (8)	124
Archie Poulton (7)	125
Daniel Watson (8)	126
Daniel Trewick (7)	127
Logan Edward Keith Miller-Hackett (8)	128
Eve Mason (8)	129
Emily Hutchinson (8)	130
Jake Taylor (8)	131

Lemington Riverside Primary School, Lemington

James Cooper (7)	132
Eve Porter (7)	133
Lexus Carter (8)	134
Megan Oetting (9)	135
Ryan Johnson (8)	136
Brooke Mavis Crombie (7)	137
Brawley Kenzie-Lee Thomson (8)	138
Lacey May Loder (8)	139
Mya Kelly (7)	140
Crystal Daglish (8)	141
Annalise Forster-Minto (7)	142
Leon Lye (9)	143
Kiki Alex Rossen (8)	144
Isobel Eve James (8)	145

Newbottle Primary School, Newbottle

Megan Young (10)	146
Summer Christie (8)	147
Charlie Piper (9)	148
Lennon Samuel Colley (9)	149
Tilly May Lydiatt (9)	150
Isla Ramshaw (8)	151
Finlay James Lowes (7)	152

Oxclose Primary Academy, Oxclose

Logan Walton (10)	153
Simone Crampton (10)	154
Ella Lee (10)	156
Abigail Joan Hill (10)	158
Leon Aiken-Saville (9)	160
Alannah Peaches Taylor (9)	161
Mia Barrett (10)	162
Emily Thornton (9)	163
Ruby Cochrane (10)	164
Bethany Rickard (10)	165
Lucas McGuire (10)	166
Tieran Gawthorpe (9)	167
Joe Kent (9)	168
Finn Nelson (9)	169
Laiton Potts (9)	170
Phillip Scott (10)	171
Emily Jordinson (10)	172
Leon Solomon (10)	173
Lucy Smith (10)	174

The Beacon Centre, South Shields

Kyle Medhurst (9)	175
Lucas Green (8)	176
Kaiden Moss (7)	177

THE POEMS

Christmas Fun

A sense of Christmas is in the air...
I see cotton snow falling from the sky
Waiting to be played with by the children nearby.
I hear Santa laughing all happy and jolly,
While Christmas cakes
Are topped with festive holly.
I smell turkey roasting for the dinner,
First to clear their plate is the winner!
I taste hot chocolate on my tongue,
Because I cleared my plate, hooray I won!
A gift is given, I feel paper rip,
Back to my hot chocolate I take a little sip.
Merry Christmas to all
And a good night,
Hoping all of your Christmases
Are festive and white.

Grace Slesser (10)
Harton Primary School, South Shields

Dream Land

Dream Land is the place to be
If you want to come just follow me.
All your dreams will come true
And no one will ever hurt you.
If you try the apple pie
You won't tell a single lie.
All your dreams will fall from the sky
And they will never say goodbye.
The penguin's feet are floppy
And they will make you happy.
The animals here are cute
And they even wear boots.
The children here in this land
Are very lovely and grand.
The fish swim gracefully
And the kids watch carefully.

Imogen Wilson (8)
Harton Primary School, South Shields

Horror Land

This place is not a joke,
Burning brains and lots of smoke.
Skeletons, blood, zombies and an oak,
You'll only hear a little croak,
The loudest person who spoke was the only good folk.
There will be a little lightning stroke,
When they start to talk.
This place only has baths of blood
No, get prepared if you want to know.
Rainbows and unicorns aren't here
Everyone here is almost broke.
Only a few can actually walk
This is what the dead has woke.
Only one person wears a cloak.

Millie Elizabeth Merrigan (9)
Harton Primary School, South Shields

Mythical Mountain

At Mythical Mountain,
There's a chocolate fountain.
If you don't like meat
Come and get a treat.

I got a lolly
With my best friend, Molly.
There's a chocolate river
Where the jellyfish glimmer.

There's a magical candy cane
That will give you no pain.
The mountain is made out of sugar,
Come if you're a sweet lover.

Come and get a gummy worm
Otherwise you will squirm.
Come and find it
Otherwise you might get hit.

Caitlyn Dalton (9)
Harton Primary School, South Shields

Candy Land!

Candy Land is very grand,
As all the sweets fall into my hand.
When I'm walking by all I see,
Is sugar and candy surrounding me.
Pink, yellow, blue, it's all so bright,
Candy Land is an amazing sight.
If I could go anywhere for just one day,
Candy Land is where I'd stay.
Candyfloss clouds and a chocolate lake
Which you can cross on a Cadbury's Flake.
Come with me and you'll see
That Candy Land is the place to be!

Keira Start (10)

Harton Primary School, South Shields

Aqua Land

Aqua Land is the place to be,
Just dive right in and you will see;
Wonderful, whirring whirlpools swirl,
Magical, mystic mermaids twirl.

Fantastic, friendly fish glide,
While slippery sea snakes hide,
In the amazing aqua atmosphere,
Silently smiley sharks you will not fear.

Sparkling, shimmering shells so bright,
Treasure troves tucked away from sight,
Just dive right in and you will see,
Aqua Land is the place to be.

Daniel Allen (9)
Harton Primary School, South Shields

Easter Island

Come to Easter Island,
Where the boys and girls play.
Come to Easter Island,
Every single day.

Eat all the candy,
Eat all the sweets.
No beach, nothing sandy,
Hear the birds tweet.

Picture this place,
With kids making a fuss.
Let them stuff their face,
Nothing at all to suss.

Come to Easter Island,
Where all the rabbits hop.
Come to Easter Island,
No sweets shall rot!

Amie De Matas (9)
Harton Primary School, South Shields

Dream Land

A place where dreams come true
And you never feel blue.
Perhaps it could sherbet rain
Or you could wish for fame
Or say that aliens came.
Ice cream for breakfast, dinner and tea
Guess what - it's free!
Be kind, that makes you cool
That's the number one rule.
Dream Land here I come,
I'm waiting for tons of fun.

Lily Ava Bell (9)
Harton Primary School, South Shields

Whale World

W hales, whales everywhere, they're even over there!

H appy whales swimming free

A ll around there are big booming sounds

L urking through the clouds of krill

E very whale is on its move to find some yummy food

S ome are small, some are big, however all are living in big, blue, wonderful Whale World.

Ava-Suri Rowell (10)

Harton Primary School, South Shields

Fairy Land

Fairy Land is always fun
No one there is ever glum,
Fairies are kind
Not a nasty one you'll find.

All the other lands arc bitter
Fairy Land is filled with glitter,
It's pretty and magical there
With beautiful shiny colours everywhere.

They love to eat trifle
They find it very joyful.

Chloe Harris (9)
Harton Primary School, South Shields

Cheerleader

C heer is the place to be,

H ot spot on the floor, marking the place I have to be,

E ars hearing the beat and body feeling the rhythm

E nding in sight and cheerleaders awarding,

R esting for a while until the next time round.

Leila Dickinson (10)

Harton Primary School, South Shields

Dragon's Land

Dragons fly
In the blue sky.
The towers are high
In the blue sky.
At night the stars glow
And watch you when you grow.
Dragons fly,
Oh my!
The time flies by
Because you're having fun.
Climb, climb to the jewelled sky.

Emily Beales (10)
Harton Primary School, South Shields

The Sweet Candy Adventure

Sweet gumdrops fall from the sky
One girl comes over and decides to say 'hi'.
A huge waterfall of chocolate
As it splashes upon the grass
Another little girl decides to come and pass
Giant lollies swing through the sky
As small cherries slowly pass by
Two little girls find a house
And in the house they found a chocolate mouse.
As tiny sweets fall down
A little girl found a gummy crown
As all the sweets fall and make a Mickey
Slowly a tiny city forms
A little bit of sugar rush
Makes a little candy bush
All of those things make our sweet candy
adventure.

Angel Young (10)
Hebburn Lakes Primary School, Hebburn

Dreams Will Be True

D o your best to make dreams
R eal dreams may come true
E very day is dreamy
A fter they dream they may come true
M ake your dreams come true
S leep for dreams all night

W e love dreams
I will dream for everything
L ike dreams
L ove dreams

B ecome a dreamer
E very day it is dreamful

T rue to be a dreamer
R eally dreams come true
U se dreams together
E verything you do you dream.

Lauren Crawford (10)
Hebburn Lakes Primary School, Hebburn

The Candy Land Where Your Dreams Come True

In a beautiful place...

T here is a river where the gummy snakes slither.
H ere is the place where everybody comes.
E verything is extra special and pretty

C ream fills the balloons.
A beautiful candy shop.
N eed some fun come right here
D o you want to see the best rainbow, see the magic candyfloss rainbow?
Y ou need to come here to have some fun.

Sophie Ellie Anderson (10)

Hebburn Lakes Primary School, Hebburn

Underwater City

U nder the sea there's lots of fun
N o evil far under the sea
D eep, deep down the kingdom lies
E els swim happily along the seashore
R oars of happiness every day
W aves splash, cheerful all the time
A res swings his wand, making it rain candy
T ime to make us grateful
E els sing as the waves splash
R ain of water making tiny splashes.

Jake Ridley (10)
Hebburn Lakes Primary School, Hebburn

Candy City

In the candy city,
Everything's colourful.
Tasty treats for everyone,
Straight into your tummy!

There isn't just one brick,
Caramel makes it stick.
Gummy bears on the Maoam grass,
Breaking up with a lot of joy.

The trees are still green
But they're filled with cream.
Everybody's welcome to see
The wonderful cream from out the stream!

Tristan Jennings (10)
Hebburn Lakes Primary School, Hebburn

Dreams

D elightful dreams
R unning through
E veryone's mind
A nd they
M ay come to life
S ilently

Birds humming across the calm blue sky
Dreams flying around, searching for someone
Sweet grass swaying in the wind
And children eating candy.

Jessica Mcelwee (9)

Hebburn Lakes Primary School, Hebburn

The Pirate And The Robot Help The Child

P irates helping the land
I n the house the child was scared
R obots are controlling the laser bot
A nd the cannon is about to shoot
T he creature is still moving
E veryone is trying to save the child
S lowly the creature goes floppy and dies.

Ben McIntyre (10)
Hebburn Lakes Primary School, Hebburn

Minecraft

In Minecraft
You mine and craft while having fun,
But sometimes you might run.
In the night you might sleep,
But sometimes you might leap.
Sometimes you might keep
But sometimes you might eat.

Callum Thomas Alder (9)
Hebburn Lakes Primary School, Hebburn

Delicious Candy

C ome to my land of candy.

A nd have an amazing time.

N ow pick a treat from my amazing sweet shop.

D elicious sweets for you and me.

Y ummy, delicious treats, get your favourite.

Alisha May Dixon (9)

Hebburn Lakes Primary School, Hebburn

Candy Land

C andy is yummy

A nd it's an amazing treat

N atural sweet to eat

D elicious candy - you should eat

Y ou love candy, I love candy, we all love candy!

Lily-Jo Shippen (10)
Hebburn Lakes Primary School, Hebburn

Nightmare City

Nightmare City,
No colour at all.
Blackness,
Creaking and scratching surrounds you.
But who's creeping around?
Who could it be?
Blood notes on windows
Run, help!

Liam Jobling (9)
Hebburn Lakes Primary School, Hebburn

Candy Animal Land!

C andy is sweet

A mazing treats

N atural taste in things you eat

D elicious makes in candy you take

Y es, candy is good, wouldn't you agree?

Breez Griffiths (10)

Hebburn Lakes Primary School, Hebburn

All You Can Eat World

In All You Can Eat World you will not starve.
There is lots of meat to carve.
There are lots of delicious chips,
They will give you helpful tips.

Oh I love my motorbike
But believe me, it will strike.
There is lovely green grass,
When the sun shines on the trees
It looks like garden peas.

When you eat the river
You will get a shiver.
With the gravy boat you will need a moat.

Leo Dunn (9)
Hedworthfield Primary School, Hedworth

Ocean Waves

O tters dance and prance
C urrents swirl and glide around
E els sneak and slither
A shark stalks its prey
N arwhals yawn and start to fight

W hales have a big appetite
A turtle swims so gracefully
V elvet fish swimming over me
E arth is mostly water
S o it's best we love her.

Kaci-Lea Clifford (11)
Hedworthfield Primary School, Hedworth

Pirates' Revenge

There's no break,
Just a lake for you to jump in
So you may break the law
But it will pay you a chore
So watch out for what's coming.
Pirates lurk around the sea
So if you dare come and join me.
You may sit in my chair,
I won't care as long as you give it back.
So don't be late to go on a date
With hook or that.

Ava Teresa Kennedy (8)
Hedworthfield Primary School, Hedworth

Handy Candy Land

In this land it is full of sweets,
Everyone comes to get their sugary treats.
Trees made of caramel, houses made of gum,
Biscuit clouds where they rain crumbs.

As you pick up a candy tree
Your heart beats,
When you walk down the street
There are gooey chocolate seats,
Come to handy Candy Land quick,
You won't be homesick!

Jack Kent (9)
Hedworthfield Primary School, Hedworth

Bedtime Is Scary

N ight and dawn, nightmares come,
I n the darkness your nightmares come alive.
G ive in or get out,
H ide and seek,
T rick or treat,
M ysterious land,
A ll your dreams come alive.
R IP if you die,
E nter your wildest dreams,
S cream out loud.

Jessica Brown (10)
Hedworthfield Primary School, Hedworth

Soft Snow World

All around is soft, fluffy snow,
Lots of snowballs to throw,
If you see there's floating bricks,
You may do some tricks.

Instead of houses there are snow caves,
Jump in the ice-cold river and ride the waves,
As you see there's no hassle,
Plus there is a big icicle castle.

Charlie Fairminer (10)
Hedworthfield Primary School, Hedworth

Rainbow Land

Red is a ruby-red racing car.
It is wiggly, wobbly and scrumptious.
Strawberry jelly.
Orange is tasty toffee with a creamy centre.
I can hear an orange cat miaowing.
Yellow is a frog jumping around the pond.
Green is leaves falling from the tall tree.
Blue is the sea shining brightly.

Grace Allen (7)
Hedworthfield Primary School, Hedworth

Zombie Land

Zombie Land looks like
a booby trap, hard and invisible.
Zombie Land smells like
blood, poisoned and vicious.
Zombie land tastes like
flesh, dripping with blood.
Zombie Land feels like
glass, broken and sharp.
Zombie Land sounds like
a lion's roar, loud and clear.

Ryan Eric Hall (9)
Hedworthfield Primary School, Hedworth

Candy Land

I can taste smooth caramel
running across my tongue.
I can see the chocolate river
swirling around the park.
I can touch the candy cane lamp post.
I can hear the rumble of the car,
made out of toffees, driving past.
I can smell the delicious scent
of melting chocolate.

Reece Mooney (9)
Hedworthfield Primary School, Hedworth

Candy Land

In Candy Land it's full of treats.
Marshmallow clouds you have to meet.
Skittle rainbows all bright and colourful.
Red, yellow, orange, green and blue,
Everywhere what a beautiful sight.
Coke streams and towers, everything is the best.
In Candy Land, come on down for a rest.

Owen Fothergill (9)
Hedworthfield Primary School, Hedworth

Dancing Land

Dancing Land looks like a rainbow,
bright and sunny.
Dancing Land smells like a flower,
pretty and wonderful.
Dancing Land tastes like ice cream,
minty and fresh.
Dancing Land feels like a shirt,
silky and crisp.
Dancing Land sounds like music,
dance to the beat!

Logan Mellish (10)
Hedworthfield Primary School, Hedworth

Rainbow

Red is ruby-red, creamy strawberry cake.
Strawberry ice cream with monkeys' blood.
Orange is a bright orange Sharpie
And sour orange juice.
Yellow is drizzling, dripping honey.
Green is grainy, glittery grass.
Blue is dolphins diving deep in the dark blue sea.

Lara Jo Newman (8)
Hedworthfield Primary School, Hedworth

Skateboard Land

I can see skateboards whizzing around, speeding in the skate park.
You can feel smooth ramps under your wheels.
You can smell a delicious McDonald's Big Mac.
You can hear skateboard wheels railing in the park.
You can taste Chicken Legends after a long day.

James Trainer (8)
Hedworthfield Primary School, Hedworth

Candy Land

I hear toffee apples falling
from the candyfloss trees.
I can see delicious chocolate raindrops falling.
I can smell the beautiful gingerbread house.
I can taste the big sweet chocolate puddles.
I can touch the soft bouncy marshmallow path.

Cody Griffiths (7)
Hedworthfield Primary School, Hedworth

Rainbow Land

Red is blood.
It is fire engines.
It is being loved.
Orange is loud, noisy turkeys.
Yellow is golden, crispy chips on a sunny day.
Blue is a dolphin.
Purple is thistles in a forest.
Pink is a baby pig's nose.

Lola Rae Wigglesworth (7)
Hedworthfield Primary School, Hedworth

Magic Land

Magic Land looks like a rainbow, sparkling in the sky.
It smells like sticky, pink candyfloss.
It sounds like bells ringing noisily.
It tastes like a crackly Crunchie bar.
Magic Land feels like sparkly, soft and fluffy clouds.

Jordan Shaw (9)

Hedworthfield Primary School, Hedworth

Llama Land

Llama Land is incredible,
Llamas run wildly
And party all night.
Music plays as they dance and prance,
Always happy.

Llama Land is amazing,
Animals can talk,
Never-ending fun,
Disco till you drop.

Tammie Shauna McDermott Hull (9)
Hedworthfield Primary School, Hedworth

Death Land

Death Land looks dark and miserable.
Death Land smells like burning, flaming lava.
Death Land tastes like smoke and burnt bones.
Death Land feels like a red hot desert.
Death Land sounds like volcanoes erupting.

Rafal Dobosz (11)
Hedworthfield Primary School, Hedworth

Animal World

A nimals are very playful
N aughty sometimes
I n and out
M onkeys climb from tree to tree
A nimals big and small
L ovely puppies play together.

Kyle Goddard (10)

Hedworthfield Primary School, Hedworth

Doughnut Land

I can hear the jam river splashing.
I can see the doughnut sun shining.
I can smell the delicious doughnut trees.
I can taste the soft sweet doughnuts.
I can touch the wet jam river.

Logan Hugh Patterson (8)
Hedworthfield Primary School, Hedworth

The Sea Tree

Deep underwater is a phenomenal sea tree,
It is the weirdest thing you will ever see.
The fish are playful and they sway through,
In the branches there are octopus tentacles
grabbing you.

Adam Roberts (10)
Hedworthfield Primary School, Hedworth

The Doggy Land

I see dogs playing with a ball.
I can touch fluffy, cute dogs.
I can smell the wet puppies.
I can hear the dogs barking for food.
I can taste the dog food in the air.

Lily Kay Newman (9)

Hedworthfield Primary School, Hedworth

Ice Cream Land

I can see delicious ice cream.
I can hear people eating.
I can smell the chocolate sauce river.
I can touch the crunchy cones.
I can taste sweet monkey blood.

Mikey Compton (7)
Hedworthfield Primary School, Hedworth

Rainbow Land

I can hear colourful rain.
I can see beautiful rainbows.
I can smell gold at the end of the rainbow.
I can taste the Skittles.
I can touch the rainbow.

Taylor Jay Harwood (8)
Hedworthfield Primary School, Hedworth

Fortnight

Running swiftly in my scary, outstanding and
breathtaking fantasy land,
I will catch a glimpse of an outstanding
extraordinary RPG quickly whizzing in the air.

Running swiftly in my scary, outstanding and
breathtaking fantasy land,
I will catch a glimpse of a violent, speedy and flying
bullet shot.

Hiding scared in my brilliant, amazing and
fantastic fantasy land,
My nose will smell a horrible black, toxic, extra
large puff of stinky smoke which will sting my eyes.

Running energetically I will be so determined to
escape the extraordinary storm before me
Shaking nervously my heart would be beating
vigorously.
My ears will be sore from the breaking brick and
straight brown buildings,
Stacking on top of each other, extremely fast and
furious.

Beautiful, gentle breeze whistling calmly.

Grayson Fenwick (7)
Hill View Junior School, Sunderland

Candy Land

Running cautiously in my spectacular, colourful
and fantastic fantasy land,
I will gaze at an unbelievable, outstanding candy
castle, swaying violently in the powerful wind.

Running cautiously in my spectacular, colourful
and fantastic fantasy land,
I will gaze at a delicious, yummy cupcake waiting
patiently to be eaten!

Walking gracefully in my tropical, delightful and
magnificent fantasy land,
I will smell the fragrance of an awesome, lovely,
minty ice cream, falling off the cone, because it is
melting.

Walking gracefully in my tropical, delightful and
magnificent fantasy land,
I will smell the fragrance of a creamy, crunchy,
wonderful chocolate bar,
crumbling because somebody ate a little nibble.

Standing darkly in my incredible, unbelievable,
magnificent fantasy land,

I will pay attention to the sound of a dazzling, brilliant bird
singing so beautifully with its fabulous voice.

Standing darkly in my incredible, unbelievable and magnificent fantasy land,
I will pay attention to the sound of colossal dropping dangerously from a house roof because the roof is breaking.

Isla Jewitt (7)
Hill View Junior School, Sunderland

Sugar Rush

Walking merrily in my fantastic, incredible and
beautiful fantasy land,
I will gaze at an excellent, outstanding Coca-Cola
volcano, exploding onto the spectacular candy
trees.

Walking merrily in my fantastic, incredible and
beautiful fantasy land,
I will gaze at an unbelievable, fluffy candy castle,
swaying over a dazzling chocolate house.

Standing quietly in my peaceful, delightful and
tropical fantasy land,
my nose will smell an intelligent, brilliant racer,
learning to drive an amazing race car.

Standing quietly in my peaceful, delightful and
tropical fantasy land,
and my nose will smell an intelligent, brilliant
chocolate race track,
that is waiting to be eaten.

Lying comfortably in my magical, smooth and shimmering fantasy land,
I will listen to the gleaming, graceful candy cane growing enthusiastically up to the sky.

Lying comfortably in my magical, smooth and shimmering fantasy land,
I will listen to the awesome, magnificent chocolate river flowing away to a far away land.

Aryssa Dania Izam (7)
Hill View Junior School, Sunderland

Robloxia

Running swiftly and amazingly in my colourful,
magical and outstanding fantasy land,
I will gaze at the amazing, adventurous, magical
powers that are trying to get in the magnificent
castle.

Running swiftly and amazingly in my colourful,
magical and outstanding fantasy land,
I will gaze at the amazing and adventurous world
of Goku simulator, Goku is defeating the dark lord.

Lying quietly and gracefully in my beautiful,
delightful and gleaming fantasy land,
my nose will smell a flaming marshmallow, it is
tropical popical.

Lying quietly and gracefully in my beautiful,
delightful and gleaming fantasy land,
My nose will smell a hot dog sizzling deliciously.

Walking softly and peacefully in my excellent,
breathtaking and adorable fantasy land,
I will listen to a beautiful, intelligent bird singing in
the simulator as they are flying.

Walking softly and peacefully in my excellent,
breathtaking and adorable fantasy land,
I will listen to a beautiful, intelligent bug crawling
everywhere.

Sebastian Cowie (8)

Hill View Junior School, Sunderland

Star Wars Land

Running nervously in my incredible, fantastic and awesome fantasy land,
I will catch a glimpse of a menacing, breathtaking top secret base quickly camouflaging in the moonlight.

Running nervously in my incredible, fantastic and awesome fantasy land,
I will catch a glimpse of a spaceship quickly zooming off towards the planet's light.

Walking majestically in my delightful, magical and peaceful fantasy land,
my nose will smell a despicable and evil machine that wickedly shreds people in half.

Walking majestically in my delightful, magical and peaceful fantasy land,
my nose will smell a despicable and evil room that has saws and chops your arms in half.

Standing excitedly in my amazing, energetic and breathtaking fantasy land,

I will listen to the outstanding and brilliant lightsabers clashing together.

Standing excitedly in my amazing, energetic and breathtaking fantasy land,
I will listen to the brilliant and outstanding laser guns shooting the evil villains wildly.

Owen Noble (8)
Hill View Junior School, Sunderland

Minecraft

Running quickly in my fantastic, unbelievable and awesome fantasy land,
I will gaze at an outstanding and brilliant creeper walking gracefully in the distance.

Running quickly in my fantastic, unbelievable and awesome fantasy land,
I will gaze at an excellent and peaceful village standing in the sunlight.

Walking delightfully in my adventurous, amazing and extraordinary fantasy land,
my nose will smell the lively and intelligent pig running wildly in the forest.

Walking delightfully in my adventurous, amazing and extraordinary fantasy land,
My nose will smell an adventurous and magnificent cow plodding gladly.

Jogging enthusiastically in my magical, spectacular and breathtaking fantasy land,
I will pay attention to the sound of an amazing and wild parrot flying beautifully.

Jogging slowly in my magical, spectacular and breathtaking fantasy land,
I will pay attention to the sound of the river thrashing against the hills.

Ben Lusby (7)
Hill View Junior School, Sunderland

Fairyland

Running swiftly in my magical, beautiful and
dazzling fantasy land,
I will gaze at an outstanding and spectacular fairy
castle standing gracefully on a hill.

Running swiftly in my magical, beautiful and
dazzling fantasy land,
I will gaze at an outstanding and elegant wizard's
house standing peacefully on a snowy mountain.

Walking majestically in my epic, peaceful and
brilliant fantasy land,
I will sniff at an awesome and lovely rosy breeze
blowing in the air.

Walking majestically in my epic, peaceful and
brilliant fantasy land,
I will sniff at an awesome and lovely summer air
going wild.

Sitting happily in my adventurous, magnificent and
unbelievable fantasy land,
my ears will hear an amazing and extraordinary
fairy flapping her wings in the sky.

Sitting happily in my adventurous, magnificent and unbelievable fantasy land,
my ears will hear an amazing and extraordinary fairy swishing her wings smoothly.

Lily Donaldson (7)

Hill View Junior School, Sunderland

Roblox

Running madly in my awesome, brilliant and colourful fantasy land,
I will gaze at an adventurous, magnificent Roblox maze waving gently in the wind.

Running madly in my awesome, brilliant and colourful fantasy land,
I will gaze at an extraordinary pizza place standing in the frozen white snow.

Walking slowly in my fantastic, awesome and incredible fantasy land,
I will sniff at a spectacular and tropical pizza smelling delicious.

Running madly in my awesome, brilliant and colourful fantasy land,
I will sniff at a spectacular and magnificent burger in the hotel restaurant being eaten by the excited customers.

Sitting quietly in my magical, magnificent and smooth fantasy land,
I and my friends will hear cars starting their engines loudly like a dinosaur roaring.

Sitting quietly in my magical, magnificent and smooth fantasy land,
My ears will hear pizza being cooked in the oven by the clever cooks.

Thomas Galbarth (8)
Hill View Junior School, Sunderland

Crop Kingdom

Running swiftly in my incredible, extraordinary and amazing fantasy land
I will gaze at an outstanding, magical castle,
Standing quietly in the moonlight.

Running swiftly in my incredible, extraordinary and amazing fantasy land
I will gaze at an energetic, adventurous, minute boy running quickly while flying a kite.

Sitting silently in my spectacular, excellent and graceful fantasy land
My nose will smell the bitter, sickening smoke floating slowly into the sky.

Sitting silently in my spectacular, excellent and graceful fantasy land
My nose will smell the foul, filthy moat travelling around the castle.

Standing weakly in my unbelievable, magnificent and beautiful fantasy land
I will listen to all the knights battling loudly and dangerously.

Standing weakly in my unbelievable, magnificent and beautiful fantasy land
I will listen to the king shouting orders to all of his fearful people.

Otis Arkley (8)
Hill View Junior School, Sunderland

Hogwarts

Running excitedly in my magical, joyful and
beautiful fantasy land,
I will gaze at an outstanding and breathtaking girl
called Hermione and Ron a gooey, horrible
monster.

Running excitedly in my magical, joyful and
beautiful fantasy land,
I will gaze at a dazzling and glistening Hermione's
wand near the pond.

Walking gracefully in my shimmering, brilliant and
gleaming fantasy land,
I will sniff at the tasty and extraordinary feast.

Walking gracefully in my shimmering, brilliant and
gleaming fantasy land,
I will sniff at the steamy and smoky smoke from
the scary woods.

Climbing adventurously in my wizard, witch and
unbelievable fantasy land,
I will pay attention to the sound of the monster
that was goopy and loud.

Climbing adventurously in my wizard, witch and unbelievable fantasy land,
I will pay attention to the crazy and energetic cheering for Harry playing Quidditch.

Isabella Peacock (7)

Hill View Junior School, Sunderland

The Frozen Winterland

Walking gracefully in my brilliant, amazing and lovely fantasy land,
I will gaze at an incredible and gleaming igloo, glistening in the moonlight.

Walking gracefully in my brilliant, amazing and lovely fantasy land,
I will gaze at an outstanding and dazzling fountain shimmering in the sunlight.

Running joyfully in my spectacular, unbelievable and peaceful fantasy land,
My nose will smell the excellent and brilliant steak cooking above the fire.

Running joyfully in my spectacular, unbelievable and peaceful fantasy land,
My nose will smell the awesome and magnificent chicken roasting on a wire.

Sitting cheerfully in my magical, sensational and tropical fantasy land,
I will listen to the burning sound of the fire flickering.

Sitting cheerfully in my magical, sensational and tropical fantasy land,
I will listen to the people talking loudly in the frozen igloo.

Benjamin Clark (8)

Hill View Junior School, Sunderland

Jungle City

Walking excitedly in my adventurous, tropical and magnificent fantasy land,
my eyes will see a sparkling, dazzling river moving swiftly across the jungle.

Walking excitedly in my adventurous, tropical and magnificent fantasy land,
my eyes will see an unbelievable, amazing tree dazzling beautifully in the sunlight.

Sitting sweetly in my lovely, peaceful and extraordinary fantasy land,
my nose will smell the tasty, delicious fruit growing in the jungle.

Sitting sweetly in my lovely, peaceful and extraordinary fantasy land,
my nose will smell the leafy fresh mint growing all around.

Kneeling gracefully in my spectacular, awesome and fantastic fantasy land,
my ears will hear the amazing sound of a parrot squawking loudly.

Kneeling gracefully in my spectacular, awesome and fantastic fantasy land,
my ears will hear the river flowing crazily here and there.

Ava Fox (7)
Hill View Junior School, Sunderland

Roblox Life

Running quickly in my magical, excellent and
unbelievable fantasy land,
I will stare at the magnificent and awesome weight
lifting champion lifting weights strongly.

Running quickly in my magical, excellent and
unbelievable fantasy land,
I will stare at a heavy and tropical weight shining
in the sun.

Skipping dreamily in my adventurous, colossal and
beautiful fantasy land,
I will sniff at the fresh and sweet air blowing
around everywhere.

Skipping dreamily in my adventurous, colossal and
beautiful fantasy land,
I will sniff at the unbelievable and magnificent air,
circling everywhere.

Sitting peacefully in my sunny, adorable and
amazing fantasy land,
my ears will hear the deep breaths howling angrily.

Sitting peacefully in my sunny, adorable and amazing fantasy land,
my ears will hear an angry voice everywhere.

Luca Zakaidze (8)
Hill View Junior School, Sunderland

The Prince's Kingdom

Running quickly in my delightful, crowded and busy fantasy land.
I will catch a glimpse of a tall and incredible prince, sitting elegantly in a tower. Gazing at the copper statue in the hillside below the shining sunset.

Sitting joyfully, delightfully and comfortably in my fantasy land.
I will smell the fragrance of the sensational and graceful onion rings, cooking magnificently.

Lying peacefully in my sensational, breathtaking and glistening fantasy land.
I will listen to the beautiful and dazzling birds cheeping.

Sitting dreamily in my intelligent, outstanding and amazing fantasy land.
I can feel the comfy and incredible sofa sitting comfortably in the flowery field.

Kneeling excitedly in my loud, lively and magical fantasy land.
My ears can hear the noisy and sizzling river thrashing wildly around the bend.

Max Kelly (7)
Hill View Junior School, Sunderland

Six Nation School

S ix Nations has started now.

I taly's kicker misses.

X ylophone cheering loudly in the crowd.

N ever before has Gary Hill scored.

A merica Vs England in the final.

T im Sexton makes Ireland in the quarter final.

I reland get beaten by England.

O ther teams are the worst.

N ever before has France been so rough.

S ix tries England scored.

S everal people throw the ball as fast as lightning.

C harlie Fredman scores a try.

H air from a rugby player gets ripped off.

O riginally players that go in the scrum have mouth guards.

O ther things might be weird but it's a flying referee.

L ie on the sofa watching the Six Nations.

Euan McDermott (7)

Hill View Junior School, Sunderland

Skittle City

In Extraordinary Land I can see...
A shining Skittle sun floating
As high as Mount Everest.
Two pink, fluffy, spiralling, swirly lollipops
And candyfloss clouds as fluffy as a sheep.
Tempting terrific trees and tasty toffee apples.

In Extraordinary Land I can see...
A jumbo marshmallow hill as soft as a pillow
And a hard, bumpy Crunchie bar hill
Standing as straight as a soldier.

In Extraordinary Land I can see...
Delicious, delightful hills
Covered with swirling, spiralling lollipops.

In Extraordinary Land I can see...
A delicious jelly baby
Holding a sweet, smelly Skittle stop sign
Next to tempting, tasty chocolate bar houses
And a fascinating, mouth-watering
Rainbow belt road.

Alexandra Mia Wood (8)
Hill View Junior School, Sunderland

Chocolate Wonders

In the land of Chocolate Wonders everyone is happy.
There are lots of chocolates to nibble and bite.
Everyone is happy, especially in the night.
You can hear the relaxing river that flows majestically, you can see extraordinary chocolate rainbows.
Even the clouds are as soft as marshmallows.
In the land of Chocolate Wonders everyone is happy.
If you eat a special piece of chocolate you will fly high in the sky.
In the land of Chocolate Wonders everyone is happy,
There is a colossal castle built for the queen, but we can eat it if you are keen!
In the land of Chocolate Wonders everyone is happy.
We will have lots of fun lying peacefully under the chocolate sun.
In the land of Chocolate Wonders everyone is happy.

Florence Hodgetts (8)
Hill View Junior School, Sunderland

Candy World

Running boldly in my amazing, fantastic and lovely fantasy land,
I will stare at incredible and unbelievable candy houses swaying amongst the sugary break.

Running boldly in my amazing, fantastic and lovely fantasy land,
I will stare at a beautiful and wonderful castle standing silently.

Walking elegantly in my peaceful fantasy land,
I will sniff at the fantastic and amazing candy flowers.

Jogging elegantly in my amazing, tropical and outstanding fantasy land,
I will listen to the brilliant and smooth Candy Village chattering speedily.

Jogging elegantly in my amazing, tropical and outstanding fantasy land,
I will listen to the smooth Candy Town eventually.

Matthew Jackson (8)
Hill View Junior School, Sunderland

Marshmallow Land

Sitting bravely in my sugary, beautiful and smooth fantasy land,
I will gaze at an unbelievable squishy marshmallow.

Sitting bravely in my sugary, beautiful and smooth fantasy land,
I will gaze at a fairy flying across the meadow.

Standing in my bouncy, awesome and lovely fantasy land,
I will sniff at an outstanding magical castle.

Standing in my bouncy, awesome and lovely fantasy land,
I will sniff at an outstanding fragment of frosting.

Walking in my elegant, spectacular and epic fantasy land,
I will listen to the brilliant fairy wings flapping crazily.

Walking in my elegant, spectacular and epic fantasy land,
I will listen to the dazzling, sophisticated fairy.

Abbie Rochester (8)
Hill View Junior School, Sunderland

Castle Kingdom

Sitting quietly in my tropical, breathtaking and awesome fantasy land,
my eyes will see an amazing, outstanding castle standing strongly in the firm breeze.

Sitting quietly in my tropical, breathtaking and awesome fantasy land,
eyes will see an unbelievable moat flowing quickly along the strong, rapid river.

Walking nervously in my excellent, beautiful and incredible fantasy land,
I will sniff the odour of the magnificent, dazzling, sweet smell
going through the air.

Walking nervously in my excellent, beautiful and incredible fantasy land,
I sniff the odour of the city surrounding the castle at the top of a gigantic hill.

Joshua Burton (7)
Hill View Junior School, Sunderland

Football Land

Running swiftly in my smooth, amazing and
brilliant fantasy land
My eyes will see an awesome and spectacular
football land.
I can see the awesome crowd are jumping wildly.

Running swiftly in my smooth, amazing and
brilliant fantasy land
My eyes will see extraordinary people eating all of
their sweets merrily.

Jogging playfully in my great fantasy land
My nose will smell the yummy toffee apple rising
from the sky.

Calmly running in my magnificent land
I can hear the crowd shouting, "Hit the ball!"

Calmly running in my magnificent land
I can hear the strong wind whistling wildly.

Harry Naill Richardson (7)
Hill View Junior School, Sunderland

The Secret Land

T he joyful, peaceful fish swam across the lake.

H ouse standing proudly next to the deep, dark lake.

E normous houses standing together.

S ecret tree house standing by the lake.

E normous, incredible rainbow randomly up in the sky.

C alm fish swimming by gracefully.

R ainbow fish swam blissfully.

E ven the sky shone light up above.

T wo people crossing the bridge over the lake.

L eaves flying excitedly by.

A nd it was Christmas time.

N ear the houses stands a beautiful castle.

D angerous fish swimming by.

Kyle Austin (8)
Hill View Junior School, Sunderland

Sweetie City

In my sweetie city I can see...
A mouth-watering, tasty Skittle sun.
Pink, fluffy candyfloss clouds
Moving left and right.
Huge, dark chocolate hills standing strong.
Colossal, beautiful lollipops standing still.

In my sweetie city I can smell...
Tempting chocolate bars.
Sweet, sugary Skittles burning on the sun,
Long, tasty strawberry laces.
Haribo eggs.

In my sweetie city I can hear...
Candyfloss trees swaying in the wind.
Tiny, delicious chocolate people playing football.
Delicious, sugary chocolate cars
Driving over the chocolate bridge.

George Wallace (8)
Hill View Junior School, Sunderland

Scrumptious Candy Land

In my scrumptious candy land I can see...
Massive marshmallow clouds floating in the sky
Like snowflakes in the blue, green sky.
Magnificent M&Ms shimmering in the breeze.
Flying sherbety sweeties float in the sky like birds.

In my scrumptious candy land I can see...
Yummy, popping flying saucers,
Pink, purple grass-covered hills,
Awesome toffee apples and perfect pear drops
Hanging in the trees.

In my scrumptious candy land I can see...
A sweet, sour rainbow belt road,
Joyful, jolly gingerbread houses,
A church made of eggcellent eggs.

Amy Brown (8)
Hill View Junior School, Sunderland

Sugar City

In Sugar City I can see...
Clouds made of sweet, fluffy marshmallows.
A sun made of colourful, hard,
Sweet, crunchy Skittles.
Sweet, slippy, brown chocolate
Flowing down a stream.

In Sugar City I can hear...
Chocolate beards whistling like angels.
A little gummy bear jumping like a chick.
A fizzy crocodile sleeping gently.

In Sugar City I can smell...
Minty, sweet candy canes hanging on a reel.
A milk-white chocolate tree standing like a stool.
Sweet, gentle, smooth Willy Wonka chocolate
Spilling and splashing.

Luke Gray (7)
Hill View Junior School, Sunderland

Dart World

Running slowly in my magical, extraordinary and happy fantasy land
I will stare at the bouncy, colossal trampoline standing in a round dartboard.

Walking around in my beautiful, tropical, comfortable fantasy land
My nose will smell all magical things that make me nervous.

Kneeling excited in my outrageous, fantastic and peculiar fantasy land
I will listen to birds tweeting in the peaceful trees.

Kneeling excited in my outrageous, fantastic and peculiar fantasy land
Which looks extraordinary and incredible before me.

Jack Warnaby (7)
Hill View Junior School, Sunderland

Sweety Land

In my sweety land I can see...
Fluffy, colourful, bright, rainbow
Marshmallow clouds waving side to side.
Multicoloured lollipops standing
On colourful rainbow belts
And a bright yellow sun
That glows in the midday heat.

In my sweety land I can see...
Huge, bright rainbows coming together.
Tempting toffee apple sitting in the rainbow
And chocolate brick-covered houses.

In my sweety land I can hear...
Trees waving side to side in the breeze.
People talking about the cotton candy soft trees.

Sophie Rose Bell (8)
Hill View Junior School, Sunderland

Candyfloss Village

In Candyfloss Village everything is edible.
A yummy, tasty walkway made of candyfloss.
It's well and truly the best.
In Candyfloss Village you can feel the soft candy.
All soft and fluffy it is the best.
In Candyfloss Village everything is edible.
A yummy, tasty walkway made of candyfloss.
It's well and truly the best.
You can hear children laughing.
The glitter cloud is amazing.
In Candyfloss Village everything is edible.
A yummy, tasty walkway made of candyfloss.
It's well and truly the best.

Madeleine Mae Copus (7)
Hill View Junior School, Sunderland

Eat Me World

E ach world is boring but not this wonderful one.

A t Candy World you can do anything!

T hings can be bad but not here, the colourful candy will help you.

M agical things will happen here

E verything is possible at Candy World.

W ords mean nothing but candy does.

O ur candy will make you go out of this world.

R oyal palaces always have sweets.

L ittle mistakes are okay so you can still have candy

D ark pink marshmallows float over the candy trees.

Imilia Young (8)

Hill View Junior School, Sunderland

In My Candy Imaginary Land

In my candy imaginary land...
There are light, fluffy, pink candyfloss clouds
Which are as light as a feather,
Let's hope they don't blow away in bad weather.

In my candy imaginary land...
I see there is a smoking, chubby,
Heavy, melted M&M sun
As heavy as a rock
And it looks like a flaming, round block.

In my candy imaginary land...
There is a happy, jolly rainbow sour mixture
That is as sour as a tongue twister
Which you will have a mouth mixture.

Zahra Ellen Roxby (7)
Hill View Junior School, Sunderland

Candy Land

In my candy land I can see...
Soft, cuddly clouds
With winding, scrumptious lollipops inside them.
A melting, marvellous M&M sun shining bright.
Lollipops hanging around.

In my candy land I can see...
Three trees with little toffee apples,
Fluffy as cotton candy.
Sweet mouth-watering sour drop river.

In my candy land I can see...
Houses with hard, sweet chocolate tiled roofs.
A puffy, soft marshmallow trampoline.
A sticky, gooey chocolate pool.

Owen Taylor Short (7)
Hill View Junior School, Sunderland

Candy Land

It's a nice sunny day,
Not a cloud in the sky,
The flowers are looking good
As the birds flutter nearby.

Delicious, yummy lollipops
Standing deliciously.

Colourful, rainbow M&M
Toadstools looking round.

Browny, creamy chocolate lake
With chocolate waves.

Bright, small Skittles
Skipping joyously.

Chocolate candy castle
And colourful walls.

Scrumptious long KitKat
Looking delicious.

Ollie Bennett (8)
Hill View Junior School, Sunderland

Aisilund

A ll the great, green grass waves swiftly in the fields.

I nside the towering, slim hotel shouting noisily.

S o calm, lovely city centre talking quietly.

I need to go to the white, tall hospital, hurrying quickly.

L ovely, brilliant house quietly banging.

U nder the big, humongous bushes waving suddenly.

N o one dares to break the terrific, brilliant rules uncarefully.

D o remember that the amazing super city relies on you!

Abigail Fox (8)

Hill View Junior School, Sunderland

Candy Village

In Candy Village you can see the strawberry gummy bear a'hanging from the candy cane tree.
In Candy Village you can hear lovely, kind people eating crunchy, sweet candy canes.
In Candy Village people shout loudly, "Come and get candy!"
In Candy Village you can feel the very sticky toffee.
In Candy Village you can taste toffee pencil cases coming from trees.
In Candy Village you can smell the peppermint watermelons hanging dangerously on a jelly bean string.

Anya Grace Clayton (7)
Hill View Junior School, Sunderland

Untitled

In my magical candy land I can see...
A bright, rainbow, Skittle sun.
Pink and blue candyfloss clouds floated across.
Sweet lollipops lined the top of the hills.

In my magical candy land I can smell...
The glorious smell of the gingerbread man
And the amazing cinnamon river.
The fudge candy houses
And the very frosty, juice pond.
I can smell the Skittle bread.

In my magical candy land I can hear...
The really melty snowman.

Molly Imogen Greenwood (7)
Hill View Junior School, Sunderland

Candy Land

In my candy land I can see...
Pink, fluffy, tasty, delicious floss clouds
Floating like bubbles.
Cold, drizzling, bright yellow
Banana milkshake rivers.
Burning, hard, colourful M&M sun
Shining bright in the sky.

In my candy land I can see...
A dark, chocolate monkey
Screeching in the dark, gloomy chocolate trees,
Which are swaying like the wind.
In my candy land I can see...
The hot, dark chocolate of the bubbling river.

Kophie Ellen Mckay (7)
Hill View Junior School, Sunderland

Fizzy Fun City

In the Fuzzy Fun City I can see...
A delicious M&M sun
Floating in the delicious, blueberry jelly sky.
Soft, sticky, delicious pink candyfloss clouds
Covering the M&M sun.
Melted marshmallows
Covering the chocolate, tasty trees.
Lime chocolate hills shining in the distance.

In the Fuzzy Fun City I can hear...
A gingerbread man calling my name 1000 times!
The tasty sweet peppermint breeze
Blowing in my ear.

Abbie Mary Robertson (8)
Hill View Junior School, Sunderland

Rainbow Chocolate Marshmallow Town

In Rainbow Chocolate Marshmallow Town
there is lots for you to see.
There are delicious chocolates
just for you and me.
There is an amazing, delicious chocolate castle.
Do you want a Fruit Pastille?
We can eat anything because we are all VIPs!
It is a wonderful place
where you can taste the multicoloured castle
at your own pace!
There are marshmallows
as soft as any pillow,
almost as soft as lace.

Heidi Cooke (7)
Hill View Junior School, Sunderland

Ocean Valley

I can see beautiful, colourful mermaids.
I can see pleasant dolphins in the ocean.

You can hear the magnificent animals moving in the water.

In my land, it sounds like 100 violins playing elegantly.
In my land, it sounds like there are pretty creatures under the water.
In my land, I can feel lovely, colourful corals.
In my land, you can feel amazing, smooth, wavy creatures.

You can taste salty water!

Maria Efthimia Kontou-Watson (7)
Hill View Junior School, Sunderland

Football Party World

Welcome to Football Party World
There are ginormous disco balls
that are made out of gummy bears
and lamp posts made out of chewing gum.
I can hear the cool DJ's music
and the joyful singing football goals
and it is rock music.
I fall deeply into the happiness of this world.
I can taste the candy cane goals
and the salt water.
I can smell the brick on the wall
and the DJ's box of sweets.

Harry-Thomas Storey (8)
Hill View Junior School, Sunderland

Mermaid Village

In Mermaid Village you can see the gold
sand palace from miles.
It is as tall as Rapunzel's tower.
When you feel the ground it is soft and smooth.
When you take a breath you can taste mint
freshly made in the shark sweetie shop.
As soon as you step into Mermaid Village
you can smell lovely, delicious chocolate orange!
You won't regret visiting Mermaid Village
because it is as spectacular as space!

Ava Sofia Henderson (8)
Hill View Junior School, Sunderland

American Soccer Party World

Giant striped candy canes
hold up glittering disco balls.
Children bounce loudly
on multicoloured jelly baby trampolines
In American Soccer Party World.
I can hear the wind shouting in my face.
I can hear the DJ's cool music.
I can smell candy cookies cooking in the oven.
I can smell yummy, outstanding candy canes.
I can taste the red and white candy cane.
I can taste soft, sticky jelly babies.

Riley Lucas Smith (8)
Hill View Junior School, Sunderland

Candy Land

In my candy land...
Huge ice cream clouds,
M&M sun and on the hills
Stand fabulous fizzy lollies.

In my candy land...
Soft, green grass sways in the wind,
Chocolate bar trunks and candyfloss laughs.
Just before the chocolate river
Stands lovely lollipops.

In my candy land...
There's a chocolate river,
Rainbow belt track,
Chocolate pond
And chocolate homes.

Harry Nordstrom Nellis (7)
Hill View Junior School, Sunderland

The Amazing World Of Colour

In Colour World the grass is as pink as a pearl.
The sun is blue and smells like chocolate too.
You can hear music everywhere you go.
People fly in the sky, so do houses too.
Animals are the best to see
because they are spotty.
You find pink, small sweets on the grass,
yummy in my tum.
The fluffy clouds are green like an alien.
Every house has a magic door.
Have you seen the dancing bee?

Evie Hedley (7)
Hill View Junior School, Sunderland

Chocolate World

In the world of Chocolate Land
everyone can surely eat everything
and everything is brown.
Everyone is happy
because they are eating chocolate.
I can see the magnificent,
stunning chocolate castle
covered in chocolate.
"Look we are close."
In the world of Chocolate Land
Everyone is mad about chocolate.
In the world of Chocolate Land
it is always quiet like a mouse.

Marcie Laidler (8)
Hill View Junior School, Sunderland

Mermaid Town

My land is under the sea.
Everything is amazing, full of fish for you.
Ron the fish is fun to play with.
My mermaid town is helpful and nice.
At my underwater town there are lots of fish.
Down in my town there are animals.
The dolphins are amazing creatures.
Over the bridge and underwater is fun for the fish.
When it is night-time the fish do a show for us.
Now the ocean is moving slowly.

Sophie Potts (7)
Hill View Junior School, Sunderland

Sweetville

I can see a colossal, delicious river flowing joyfully.
I can see a spectacular, mouth-watering bubblegum in a gum ball dispenser.
I can see a delightful, amazing path of sweet squares walking loudly.
I can see a wonderful, tall castle full of sweets leaning elegantly.
I can smell mouth-watering, floral flowers dancing sweetly.
I can smell amazing, wonderful chocolate stones melting slowly.

Lauren Bunting (7)
Hill View Junior School, Sunderland

My Candy Land

In my candy land I can see...
Large, fluffy candyfloss clouds.
Cool, silky chocolate drops
Falling like bubbles.

In my candy land I can hear...
The yellow M&M sun crackling.
Tiny raindrops splattering
On the long gingerbread road.

In my candy land I can smell...
Sweet gingerbread houses.
Yellow M&M sun.
Sweet pink candyfloss clouds.

Tom Eron Tindle (8)
Hill View Junior School, Sunderland

Yorkie City

In my Yorkie city I can see...
Sticky and sweet chocolate puddles.
Yummy, glossy, blue candyfloss.
Colossal rainbow lollipops.

In my Yorkie city I can smell...
Melted crunchy chocolate bars.
Sticky caramel apples roasting under the sun.
Sweet strawberry lollipops standing on the hill.

In my Yorkie city I can hear...
People crunching the chocolate bars.

Katie Reid (7)
Hill View Junior School, Sunderland

Chocolate World

I can see in Chocolate World
loads of chocolate and candy to eat.
I can hear in Chocolate World
everybody munching loudly
on chocolate and candy.
I can feel the melted chocolate
running smoothly through my fingertips.
I can taste in Chocolate Land
loads of delicious chocolate.
I can smell the chocolate fountain
that is like a delicious erupting volcano.

Abbie McIlwraith (7)
Hill View Junior School, Sunderland

Raceville

In Raceville you can see the magnificent race tracks.
In Raceville you will hear the magnificent race cars.
In Raceville it feels like a smooth chocolate land.
In Raceville you can smell the strong melting chocolate.
In Raceville it is a fantastic place to be.
In Raceville you can see the fast as lightning race cars.
Do you want to go there?

Owen Lanaghan (8)
Hill View Junior School, Sunderland

Colourful Candy Land

In my colourful candy land I can see...
Pink, fluffy candyfloss clouds,
Sweet, colourful M&M sun,
Fizzy, multicoloured flying saucers.

In my colourful candy land I can hear...
Two gingerbread men chatting.

In my colourful candy land I can smell...
Sweet, rich chocolate homes,
Sticky, sweet liquorice paths.

Sophie Ann Frater (8)
Hill View Junior School, Sunderland

In My Candy Land

In my candy land...
There is a beautiful, colourful Skittle sky
Lit up by a huge M&M sun
And beautiful sugary, sour rainbow belt clouds.

In my candy land...
There are beautiful candyfloss trees
Which have lovely melted chocolate.
Delicious, fizzy, colourful rainbow
And on top sit little Jelly Tots.

Amelie Jones (7)
Hill View Junior School, Sunderland

Marshmallow Castle

In Marshmallow Castle everything is soft.
Everything here is smooth, quiet and peaceful.
Everything is colourful and fun.
Everything here tastes like sweets and chocolate
that are beautifully made.
Everything here is big or small.
Everything here is always smooth.
Here at Marshmallow Castle everything is magical!

Zac Alexander Johnson (8)
Hill View Junior School, Sunderland

The Royal Blacksmith

Large, colossal walls standing high.
The fluffy, tiny cloud sitting in the sky.
The brave, bold blacksmith ready to battle.
The large, gold dragon breezing in the wind.
The sharp, pointy sword hanging on the wall.
The hard, strong armour turning slowly.
The hot, burning blades melting quietly.

Ben Kernen (7)
Hill View Junior School, Sunderland

The Cute Cottage

It was a sunny, bright day.
With the peaceful cottage standing happily.
The attractive butterflies flew gracefully,
Past the cottage swaying,
Picturesque grass was as green as mint.
Fairies were laughing joyfully,
Having so much fun.
The tall, towering house was as tall as a giraffe.

Grace Connor (8)
Hill View Junior School, Sunderland

The Eat Me Now World!

The chubby marshmallows are very gummy
And unbelievably delicious
And the gumball castle, fun game is so cool,
Especially in the pool.
The thick and stunning chocolate river
Makes people joyfully quiver.
The minty lime grass is very tasty
So to get some you must be fairly hasty!

Ruby Rose Skaife (8)
Hill View Junior School, Sunderland

My Edible World

Large, colourful Skittles leaping down noisily.
Smooth, drippy chocolate mountain standing tastily.
Sticky, delicious, dippy doughnuts bouncing loudly.
Saucy, lacy lollipops dripping down heavily.
Sticky, chewy gummy bear toadstools moving.
Fluffy, soft, cotton candy falling silently.

Nola Thompson (8)
Hill View Junior School, Sunderland

A Candy Land

A colossal, chocolatey cookie dripping silently.
Cute, cuddly gummy bear partying slowly.
Colourful, sugary rainbow standing so beautifully.
Welcoming, lovely gingerbread house towering
imposingly.
Wibbly, wobbly jelly jiggles quickly.
Magically terrific unicorn flying delightfully.

Amber Howey (8)
Hill View Junior School, Sunderland

Ocean

O ctopus' magnificent, unusual legs moving slowly.

C olourful, bright fish swimming quickly through the waves.

E very creature you see is outstanding.

A nimals look so mesmerising to you and me.

N ear the ocean floor, you'll never want for more.

Katelyn Dowling (7)
Hill View Junior School, Sunderland

Candy Land

In my candy land I can see...
A caramel waterfall
trickling down the road like a river.
Sweet sticky candyfloss clouds
floating gracefully in a blue bubblegum sky.

In my candy land I can see...
Sweet flying saucers
racing under sugary rainbows.

William Theodore Carson (7)
Hill View Junior School, Sunderland

Goblin Land

Little, cute goblins standing silently.
Tall, pretty flowers growing noisily.
Sparkly, colourful rainbow bending beautifully.
A huge, beautiful castle standing bravely.
The green, colossal hill standing tall.
The lovely, small fish swimming peacefully.

Sam Oxberry (8)
Hill View Junior School, Sunderland

Candy Land

The huge M&M castle standing proudly.
Yummy lollipop trees standing deliciously.
The tasty cocoa river flowing loudly.
Yummy gingerbread house leaning scarily.
Tasty, small Smartie toadstool blowing quickly.
Tasty gingerbread man standing tall.

Archie Poulton (7)
Hill View Junior School, Sunderland

Candy Football World

In Candy Football World
I can see people playing with a toffee ball.
I see the bright sun shining,
as yellow as a daffodil.
I can smell the pink, hard candy.
I can hear noisy and respectful fans.
The sky is as blue as the sea.

Daniel Watson (8)
Hill View Junior School, Sunderland

Under The Sky Blue Sea

O ceans are a terrific place.
C reeping water flowing in a warm, dark cave.
E very bright animal swims through the water.
A fish can swim slowly in the ocean.
N ever see some fish in the sea.

Daniel Trewick (7)
Hill View Junior School, Sunderland

Sugar Valley

In my sugar valley I can see a...
Green, bright spaceship like a plane.
I can see a red, bright Skittle sun.
I can see a hard, brown gingerbread man.
I can see a bright, colourful green Jelly Tot
Waving in a house.

Logan Edward Keith Miller-Hackett (8)
Hill View Junior School, Sunderland

Colourful Candy Land

Large gingerbread house standing peacefully.
Gleeful, cute gummy bear dancing merrily.
Fluffy, white clouds swaying silently.
Sweet, tasty lollipop trees shining brightly.
Colourful rainbow gleaming magically.

Eve Mason (8)
Hill View Junior School, Sunderland

Cat Land

Happy, cute cat walking noisily.
Beautiful, shining stream flowing peacefully.
Tall, towering lollipop standing quietly.
Enormous, giant castle standing happily.
Lovely, small house standing quietly.

Emily Hutchinson (8)
Hill View Junior School, Sunderland

Candy Land

A big, delicious chocolate river flowing gently.
Beautiful rainbow shining brightly.
Dark grey clouds floating by slowly.
Hot burning fire flickering hotly.
Big, long candy pole standing sensibly.

Jake Taylor (8)
Hill View Junior School, Sunderland

Robloxiz City

Welcome to my city.
It's very pretty.
We've got some bubblegum.
Everyone says, "Yum!"
Give me some money
And I'll give you a special gummy!
We'll go to the shop
And get some pop.
When you drink pop
It makes you stop.
When I go to the barber shop
It makes me hop.
When I finish coffee
It makes me have a toffee.
When I have my toffee
It tastes like coffee.
When I buy a toy
It fills me with joy.

James Cooper (7)
Lemington Riverside Primary School, Lemington

Mermaid Land

M illy the mermaid,

E verybody loves her,

R eefs tickle her arms,

M illy laughs out loud,

A s she normally does,

I t makes her smile and the fish too,

D idn't you know, she shows the fish how to swim.

Eve Porter (7)

Lemington Riverside Primary School, Lemington

Rainbow Candy Land

Raining Skittles all around you,
Rainbow lollies, very sticky, sweet candy canes.
You can see candy all around you.
You can hear Skittles drop to the floor,
You can feel sticky, trickily candy.
You can smell flavours of Skittles.

Lexus Carter (8)
Lemington Riverside Primary School, Lemington

Good Angels And Bad Angels

I can smell creamy, sweet, bad pie.
I can taste cream in my mouth.
I can see the bad angel sticking out his tongue.
I can hear the bad angels cackling.
I can feel lovely, sweet flowers swaying in the breeze.

Megan Oetting (9)

Lemington Riverside Primary School, Lemington

Untitled

I can see M&Ms falling from the sky.
I can smell M&Ms cooking.
I can feel them land on my arm.
I can taste M&Ms crunching in my mouth.
I can hear M&Ms land on the ground.

Ryan Johnson (8)
Lemington Riverside Primary School, Lemington

Raining Doughnuts

I hear people gobbling up the doughnuts
with loads of joy.
I see the love beginning to load.
I smell the delicious doughnuts.
I taste the candy air.
I touch the candy cane trees.

Brooke Mavis Crombie (7)
Lemington Riverside Primary School, Lemington

Racing City

In Racing City everything is cool.
I can see cars on tracks.
I can hear bikes zooming past.
I can taste cars' gas.
I can feel car tyres coming to me.
I can smell the crowd.

Brawley Kenzie-Lee Thomson (8)
Lemington Riverside Primary School, Lemington

Unicorns

I can hear rippling candy from the glistening sky.
I can feel the sky blue air on my face.
I can smell the lovely candy.
I can see a rainbow unicorn.
I can taste creamy toffee.

Lacey May Loder (8)

Lemington Riverside Primary School, Lemington

Smiggle

If you go to Smiggle
You will have a giggle.
The sense is nice
But all the pencil cases are bright.
The air is fruity
Like a cookie.
It's very pretty.

Mya Kelly (7)
Lemington Riverside Primary School, Lemington

Love Land

L ove is the one thing everyone needs.
O verall everyone loves their loved ones.
V alentine's Day is what I love.
E veryone loves Love Land.

Crystal Daglish (8)

Lemington Riverside Primary School, Lemington

Pusheen Land

I hear mermaids in the spa
And I smell deliciousness.
I will see Pusheens,
Also I will feel smooth fur.
If you go you will taste pizza
Or something else.

Annalise Forster-Minto (7)
Lemington Riverside Primary School, Lemington

Death World

D ie or fight,

E veryone never comes back.

A fter the death in the

D ead world,

L ay down and

Y ou will really die.

Leon Lye (9)

Lemington Riverside Primary School, Lemington

Candy Land

C andy is the best

A dream full of wonder

N ever nicer

D ream of candy

Y ou've never seen anything like it.

Kiki Alex Rossen (8)

Lemington Riverside Primary School, Lemington

Toy Land

I can see fluffy toys.
I can feel soft pillows.
I can hear bouncing toys.
I can taste marshmallows.
I can smell s'mores.

Isobel Eve James (8)
Lemington Riverside Primary School, Lemington

Wonderful Things

S uper fun in this place
P owerful things you could complete
O ver the beach where in a crab
R acing to get our back tuck
T rying to be as good as Sophie Dossi,
S truggling to be the best.

A mazing place
N o healthy things just candy
D ancing under the sun now the fun has begun

C andy, oh so sweet
A hard score to beat
N o time to take a seat
D ance, dance all day long
Y ou will love it here in Sports Candy Land!

Megan Young (10)
Newbottle Primary School, Newbottle

Magic Around Land

U nicorns are colourful and real. They have fur like a cloud.

N ever say unicorns aren't real because they are.

I n Magic Around Land unicorns will be as friendly as a friend when you need help.

C olourful unicorns give you really good luck on anything.

O nly those who truly believe will get to meet a unicorn.

R ainbows are their favourite thing because they are colourful.

N ever stop believing in unicorns!

Summer Christie (8)

Newbottle Primary School, Newbottle

Pokémon Land

P okémon packed
O verloaded with adventures
K eep winning matches and never lose
É veryone is free to become a Pokémon trainer
M atches called Pokémon battles are famous
O versleeping is bad
N ever give up and keep going

L osing is only a lesson
A fter you become champion you will become famous
N o limits
D angerous Pokémon.

Charlie Piper (9)
Newbottle Primary School, Newbottle

Underwater World

U nder the waves we're safe
N ever scared because all the fish have a face
D eep down on the sea bed
E veryone rest your head
R elax at the fishy spa
W e'll go to the fishy bar
A ll are calm, the sharks are nice
T ake a bite, there's no spice
E verything is having fun
R each out for your fish dog in its bun.

Lennon Samuel Colley (9)
Newbottle Primary School, Newbottle

Wild One

Fast as lightning, teeth as sharp as knives,
Known for frightening,
As sneaky as a spy.
Do not trust them as they might lie.
Please don't think they're cute
As they have a family to salute.
Spots cover their skin,
Their prey know they aren't going to win.
Don't set foot, you may end up with a vicious cut.
Whiskers like wire,
They know who they desire.

Tilly May Lydiatt (9)
Newbottle Primary School, Newbottle

Candy Land

If you like sweets
This is the place to meet
Sugar plums here, sugar plums there
Some people have candy hair
The grass is green
And the trees are covered in cream
The rainbows are gummy
Delicious for your tummy
Rain or shine
The sweets are divine.

Isla Ramshaw (8)
Newbottle Primary School, Newbottle

Weapon Of The Old

Bows and arrows fly through the sky
Killing animals so we can survive.
Swords are violent like everyone knows.
They protect people from enemies
In a Minecraft world.
There are weapons galore.

Finlay James Lowes (7)
Newbottle Primary School, Newbottle

Candy Land

Mysterious chocolate bars floating spookily above the roof.
Huge candy canes framing windows on the walls of the houses.
Golden grass tickles your feet as it shimmers in the sunlight.
Stacks of tiny Smarties towering taller than the clouds.
Little toffee apples blowing the trees.
Candy Land is a special experience for everyone.

Gummy bears dressed in dark blue are my bodyguards.
They protect all our gummy people from the horrible, scary prickly queen.
Wondrous chocolate waterfall shining beautifully in the sunlight
Chocolate doors standing smartly in the open air.
Amazing lollipops reaching for the sky
Candy Land is a special experience for everyone.

Logan Walton (10)

Oxclose Primary Academy, Oxclose

The Story Of Candy Land

On the kitchen side is a candy land
Where gingerbread people live.
When the light goes out
Is when the magic happens.
Gingerbread comes to life
And it is daytime in Candy Land.

Cute cat clouds floating slowly
And a candy mansion that I live in.
I am sweet Simone,
I am the mayor of Candy Land.
Every day in Candy Land
I play with gingerbread gummy bears
And the cute candyfloss cat clouds.
My police force and guards are blue gummy bears,
I have the sweetest home in Candy Land.

As the happy day turns to night
Waiting for them to switch the light,
For as human night turns into day
And we all say
We'll see each other anyway tomorrow.

Oh wait, I forgot to tell you about the Geezensnorf
The grimy Geezensnorf,
He is a pile of garbage.
Really, he is made up from leftover food
Nobody likes him because he eats candy people
And is extremely jealous of us.
Last week he ate a villager's house
It has been fixed,
Nothing stays broken in Candy Land.

Simone Crampton (10)
Oxclose Primary Academy, Oxclose

Candy Land

There is a place far away,
Where everything happens.
There is nowhere else you would want to be.
Everyone loves this place.
It's Candy Land.
Yeah, yeah, yeah!
Candy Land is so cool!

No one can beat the candy shops
Selling jumbo lollipops.
The people are made of gingerbread,
Even their yummy heads.
Yeah, yeah, yeah!
There is no place like Candy Land!

The clouds are the best.
They are made from candyfloss.
The path is so cool.
It is made of rainbow drops.
Even jumbo lollipops.
Yeah, yeah, yeah!
There is no place like Candy Land.

If you love sweets
Then you can come to Candy Land.
So what are you waiting for?
Come to Candy Land!
Yeah, yeah, yeah!
There is nowhere like Candy Land!

Ella Lee (10)
Oxclose Primary Academy, Oxclose

Gummy, Yummy Land

Minty green grass.
Sticky, swirly lollipops.
Pink, smooth candy clouds,
Waving around the sky.
Chocolate fountains, falling slowly down
For people to get a drink.
This is Candy Land.
Everyone loves being there.
Whoop! Whoop! Whoop!
This place is the place I would be
Every day to eat candy.

Candy love hearts with pink everywhere.
Gingerbread men smiling at me
And smiling at each other.
Colourful sky moving around Candy Land.
Candy canes red and white,
Standing around for people to nibble on.
This is Candy Land.
Everyone loves being there.
Whoop! Whoop! Whoop!

This place I would be
Every day to eat candy.

Abigail Joan Hill (10)
Oxclose Primary Academy, Oxclose

Candy Land

Mysterious chocolate river
flowing gently down the hill.
Magical toffee apple trees
growing slowly out of the ground.
Huge egg clouds floating beautifully
above the golden grass.
Shimmering Haribo roof
standing strongly below the sun.
Small candy cane window
standing smoothly in the open air.
Mysterious chocolate river
flowing gently down the hill;
like children sliding down a slide.

Red towering lollipop plants
reaching straight for the sky.
Amazing golden chocolate egg chimney
shining mysteriously in the air.
Oh no, I forgot to tell you about the purple goblins,
they come with sweets every month.

Leon Aiken-Saville (9)
Oxclose Primary Academy, Oxclose

Above The Clouds

I know a place where magic plays,
And every day is sunny.
A waterfall drapes like a blue velvet curtain
And the candy tastes richer than honey.
Unicorns' silky fur all colours of the rainbow,
Candy houses they don't need to pay for.
I know a place where magic plays
And that place is home.

Gummy bears, blue, green and pink
Fall on clouds so light they do not sink.
Lollipops as big as boulders -
People can't reach
So they stand on their shoulders.
Rainbows covered in dazzled glaze.
Candy Land, a place where everyone plays.

Alannah Peaches Taylor (9)
Oxclose Primary Academy, Oxclose

The Life Of Candyland

Gold, sweet house standing beautifully
in this magical candy land.
Tall, eye-catching trees dancing
slowly while they stand.
Loud, magical waterfall
glowing magically in the background.
Bald, glistening rocks float amazingly
and all you can hear is their twinkling sound.
Brown, small fences
standing smartly in the ground.

Brown, crunchy gingerbread men
marching happily on cocoa powder sand.
Squishy, cute gummy bears
jumping excitedly holding hands.
Everybody enjoys enchanted Candy Land!
Do you too?

Mia Barrett (10)
Oxclose Primary Academy, Oxclose

Unicorn Sweet Land

One day a unicorn was born
With long, colourful hair,
A pink, fluffy tail
And a shimmering, golden horn.
She loves sweets so much,
She dreams of them all night.

Sweets fall from the sky all day every day,
Lollipop trees of pink and purple,
With rainbow-coloured grass
And chocolate cookies glimmering like brass.

When it rains a million sweets
A beautiful rainbow comes for the day,
It is no ordinary rainbow, it is magic
That created this land
That is called Unicorn Sweet Land.

Emily Thornton (9)
Oxclose Primary Academy, Oxclose

Under The Sea!

Little love-heart crabs
Snip and snap along the sand.
Then run up my hand.
The rainbow sits on top of the waves
As the sea monster hungrily raves.

Wiggly, stringy seaweed wobbling in the waves.
Often fish go too quickly.
They are caught by the seaweed,
Quick, it's prickly.
The seaweed hides in caves.

Beautiful coral all sitting together
It's a lovely day for sunny weather.
Where the waves are calm
The sea monster is not doing any harm,
Under the sea together.

Ruby Cochrane (10)
Oxclose Primary Academy, Oxclose

Sugar Candy Canes

I know a place that tastes delicious
Where there is no need for dishes.
With melting cakes and a chef that bakes.
There are candy canes
That are sweet not like feet.

I know a place where kings come to play every day.
I know a country in the sky
That is a long way and very high.
There is no taste like candy canes.
Delicious, delicious candy canes.

Bethany Rickard (10)
Oxclose Primary Academy, Oxclose

Computer World

Dangerous signs warning of high voltage
Friendly robots partying in the hall
Enormous lollies spinning quickly
Chocolate fans rotating their blades
Liquorice mints wrapped up neatly in paper
Electric charged hands identifying sweets
Gears turning tirelessly to move the conveyor belt
Wonderful train working for fun
Never fear, be full with cheer.

Lucas McGuire (10)
Oxclose Primary Academy, Oxclose

Candy Land

The coloured clouds like candyfloss
And loads of little colourful millions
Like tiny ants falling from the magical sky.
The swirling lollipops like spinning wheels.

Chocolate footballs like rocks.
Rainbow sour laces for the path
And a rainbow made of sour laces
To houses like soft gingerbread
Decorated with loads of sweets.

Tieran Gawthorpe (9)
Oxclose Primary Academy, Oxclose

Dream High

See Dream City in the distance... it is majestic.
I hear students talking... it is deafening.
I smell the dream pizza in the cafeteria...
It is mouth-watering.
I touch dream orbs in the dream collection...
It is amazing!
I taste the sweet taste of success...
It is encouraging.
I feel... adventurous!

Joe Kent (9)
Oxclose Primary Academy, Oxclose

Candy Land

I know a place where candy grows
and rainbows glow.
Chocolate dripping.
Finger licking.
Candy canes hanging sweetly but neatly.
Gingerbread men running - how cunning!
Lollipops standing tall - hope they don't fall!
Chocolate numbers dripping down the door
onto the floor.

Finn Nelson (9)
Oxclose Primary Academy, Oxclose

Coke

I see... a Coke river.
It is overflowing.
I hear... a Coke waterfall.
It is overpowering.
I smell... the smell of my favourite drink.
It is delicious.
I touch... the fizzy bubbles.
It feels fuzzy.
I taste... the cold liquid.
It is mouth-watering.
I feel epic!

Laiton Potts (9)
Oxclose Primary Academy, Oxclose

Chocolate Land

C hewy and soft on my tongue.
H ot chocolate bubbles.
O h, delicious!
C runchy bars, light and dark.
O verflowing with cream.
L ovely, rich and sweet.
A mazing taste!
T reats for all
E aster fun delights!

Phillip Scott (10)
Oxclose Primary Academy, Oxclose

The Haunted House

I see a spooky haunted house.
The sight is terrifying.
I hear creaking floorboards.
The sound is freaky.
I smell yucky gloop.
The smell is nauseating.
I touch secret doors.
The feeling is obscure.
I taste rotten food.
The taste is disgusting.

Emily Jordinson (10)
Oxclose Primary Academy, Oxclose

Candy World

C andy World is my favourite place.

A ll of the trees are different kinds of candy.

N owhere else has a rainbow made with delicious M&Ms

D elicious swirls and circles fill the lollipops.

Y ummy!

Leon Solomon (10)

Oxclose Primary Academy, Oxclose

Unicorn Land

I know a place with sweet pink houses
With a sugar sink standing in the daylight,
What a sight!
Giant rainbows brightly glow
But you can blow through them.
Flying unicorns sparkle as they fly by.

Lucy Smith (10)
Oxclose Primary Academy, Oxclose

Gingerbread Land

G ingerbread Land is soft.

I have candy canes that are good.

N injas bounce on a bed of marshmallows.

G ingerbread is bouncy.

E at all of the sweets - they will grow back!

R ound up the people because the sweets are good.

B eans are made of chocolate.

R ed lollipops are cherry flavoured.

E at all of the chocolate because it is good.

A touch of the candy canes will turn you sweet.

D elicious cakes fall from the sky.

L emon drops hang from the trees.

A Smartie stream runs through the land.

N ice gummy bears are filled with candyfloss.

D ancing lollipops are your friend.

Kyle Medhurst (9)

The Beacon Centre, South Shields

Animal Land

A nimal Land smells like poo.
N ow the elephants are happy.
I t looks like a happy place.
M y land is full of excitement.
A nimals are everywhere.
L ots of people like it.

L ots of smiles from people.
A nd there are apple trees to feed the animals.
N imble nanny goats bounce around.
D ucks flap around in the pond.

Lucas Green (8)
The Beacon Centre, South Shields

Football Land

You can see the crowd standing at the match.
You can touch the back for luck.
You can smell the hot dogs in the air - delicious!
You can hear the crowd go wild
when Liverpool score the winning goal.
You can taste burgers with tomato sauce.

Kaiden Moss (7)
The Beacon Centre, South Shields

YOUNG WRITERS INFORMATION

We hope you have enjoyed reading this book – and that you will continue to in the coming years.

If you're a young writer who enjoys reading and creative writing, or the parent of an enthusiastic poet or story writer, do visit our website **www.youngwriters.co.uk**. Here you will find free competitions, workshops and games, as well as recommended reads, a poetry glossary and our blog.

If you would like to order further copies of this book, or any of our other titles, then please give us a call or visit **www.youngwriters.co.uk**.

Young Writers
Remus House
Coltsfoot Drive
Peterborough
PE2 9BF
(01733) 890066
info@youngwriters.co.uk